MW01205097

IDENTITY
REVEALED

30 Days to Know Who You Are

STEPHEN BRAZZEL

WESTBOW
PRESS®
A DIVISION OF THOMAS NELSON
& ZONDERVAN

Scripture taken from the Holman Christian Standard Bible ® Copyright ©
2003, 2002, 2000, 1999 by Holman Bible Publishers. All rights reserved.

WestBow Press books may be ordered through booksellers or by contacting:

WestBow Press
A Division of Thomas Nelson & Zondervan
1663 Liberty Drive
Bloomington, IN 47403
www.westbowpress.com
1 (866) 928-1240

Because of the dynamic nature of the Internet, any web addresses or
links contained in this book may have changed since publication and
may no longer be valid. The views expressed in this work are solely those
of the author and do not necessarily reflect the views of the publisher,
and the publisher hereby disclaims any responsibility for them.

Any people depicted in stock imagery provided by Thinkstock are
models, and such images are being used for illustrative purposes only.
Certain stock imagery © Thinkstock.

ISBN: 978-1-5127-3788-2 (sc)
ISBN: 978-1-5127-3789-9 (e)

Library of Congress Control Number: 2016905854

Print information available on the last page.

WestBow Press rev. date: 04/13/2016

INTRODUCTION

The purpose of this book is to inform you and to inspire you. Over the course of the next 30 days we'll take a look at some of the biblical passages that speak to your identity as a believer. I hope to challenge how you think about yourself.

Our self-perception comes from the culture, both secular and church, and it comes through our families, our personal history or our own personality. My goal is to inspire you through a close examination of the biblical approach to self-identity. I want you to see the faults inherent in looking at your life through the wrong lens. I want you to see yourself as God sees you, both before your salvation and after it. I want you to hold tightly to the things God says about your relationship to Him and what He has done on your behalf. I want you to accept the magnificence of His grace and embrace the new identity He purchased for you on the cross.

You can probably read through this book in a few sittings, but my suggestion is that you use it as a 30 day devotional. Read one day at a time, it should take only a few minutes to complete a chapter. If you miss a day, don't worry, just pick it up the next day. Write in it. Underline it. Use the space at the end of each chapter to respond to what the Spirit is saying to you.

My prayer is that this will be a good beginning place, or a stop along the way, to a lifelong conversation you'll have with God. It is by no means the complete summation of God's Word on identity, it is just my piece to add to the conversation. Enjoy the month with Him. Let His truth wash over you.

God bless,
Stephen Brazzel

Except where noted, scriptural references are from the Holman Christian Standard Bible (HCSB).

1/30/21

DAY 1

What Do You Call Yourself?

> Don't you realize that those who do wrong will
> not inherit the Kingdom of God? Don't fool
> yourselves. Those who indulge in sexual sin, or
> who worship idols, or commit adultery, or are
> male prostitutes, or practice homosexuality, or
> are thieves, or greedy people, or drunkards, or
> are abusive, or cheat people—none of these will
> inherit the Kingdom of God. Some of you were
> once like that. But you were cleansed; you were
> made holy; you were made right with God by
> calling on the name of the Lord Jesus Christ and
> by the Spirit of our God. (1 Corinthians 6:9–11)

Rahab the Prostitute. Doubting Thomas. The thief on the cross.

You probably recognize the names and maybe even know their
stories, or at least how they received these monikers. Rahab was a
prostitute in Jericho who hid Jewish spies, protecting them from
the king of Jericho. In Joshua 2 and 6 she is called Rahab the
prostitute four times and simply Rahab only twice; even in the
New Testament she is Rahab the prostitute (Hebrews 11:31; James
2:25) to distinguish her from the other Rahabs found in Scripture

1

(Job 9:13; 26:12; Psalm 87:4; 89:10; Isaiah 30:7; 51:9; Matthew 1:5). Many remember her as a prostitute, but few may remember her acts of courage and God's provision for her.

Thomas was a twin and one of the twelve disciples, a faithful follower of Jesus who for some reason was absent when Jesus first appeared to the disciples, as recorded in John 20:19–23. When he heard of the appearance from the other ten, he expressed his famous statement of doubt: "If I don't see the mark of the nails in His hands, put my finger into the mark of the nails and put my hand into His side, I will never believe!" (John 20:25). Forever known from that point as Doubting Thomas, he was confronted by the resurrected Jesus eight days later. Jesus offered His hand and His side, and Thomas responded with one of the first statements of the deity of Christ: "My Lord and my God!" (John 20:28). It is interesting that many know to call him Doubting Thomas, but few may realize that his was one of the first recorded confirmations of Jesus's deity.

The thief was one of three hanging on a cross that day. Joining him that day were one more thief and Jesus. His name is not known; he is recalled simply as the thief. He is remembered for his cry out to Jesus: "Jesus, remember me when You come into your kingdom!" (Luke 23:42). Jesus responded with a promise: "Today you will be with me in paradise" (Luke 23:43). That promise assures those who believe and trust Jesus as Savior and Lord that there is an immediate presence with Him after death and that nothing is required for salvation beyond a faithful call to Him. This thief, in his simple request, leaves all Christendom with lessons about salvation that are spoken simply in his story.

As important and theologically significant as these individuals are in the story of faith, they are all popularly known for their mistakes and not their faith. Rahab is still called a prostitute.

Thomas is still a doubter. The thief is, well, a thief. Be assured that today, as she stands in heaven, Rahab is not called a prostitute by her heavenly Father, and Thomas is not known as the doubter, and the thief is called by his name, not by his sin.

In the passage from 1 Corinthians, Paul is clear that we all have a history. People are often called or known by what they have done wrong, not what God has made right. Everyone has committed sin, and everyone has fallen short of the glory of God. You may have been able to hide your sin from the masses, or it may be well known. Sometimes there is no way to keep it secret. An out-of-wedlock birth, a DWI conviction, a public divorce, or any other number of public transgressions cannot be hidden from others and can become the most common way others identify you. Even if it doesn't become part of your name, like Rahab the prostitute, it can last as your reputation long after you have left that lifestyle or repented of the sin.

Even worse than the public humiliation, you might feel a private shame that never leaves. You might be haunted by your own past to the point where you are unable to go forward. You may not feel worthy to serve God or to speak on His behalf to others whose sin is less public. Without the benefit of God's work and His truth on your life, your failures may define your identity for the rest of your life.

But it doesn't have to be that way. There is hope for you. Look at the verse, "some of you *were once* like that." Rahab, Thomas, and the Remembered One each found new life and hopes for an eternal future when they came to faith. This new identity is here for you also.

By faith you call on the name of the Lord and you are cleansed; you are made holy; you are made right with God. You bring to

Him all of your mess of identity, and He begins to remake you. This is your new identity!

Prayer and Notes

_____

_____

_____

_____

_____

2|1|21

DAY 2

You Know the Truth

> Jesus said to the people who believed in Him, "You
> are truly my disciples if you remain faithful to my
> teachings. And you will know the truth, and the
> truth will set you free." (John 8:31–32)

Truth is not a philosophical proposition or a theoretical claim about the workings of the world. Truth is a person. His name is Jesus.

True freedom, not merely political or societal freedom, is centered in knowing Jesus, both objectively and experientially. The beauty of Jesus's promise is that you can enjoy true freedom in any situation without changing where you live, how much money you make, or who is running the government.

To understand this freedom requires an objective knowledge of Jesus and His Word. The first thing Jesus tells these new believers is to "continue in My Word." Those who are truly His followers will continue to learn and follow His Word. He is not saying that you gain salvation by studying His Word but that you show your salvation by spending time in His Word. This is a call to knowledge, to understanding objective truth. You must seek more knowledge of Jesus through His Word. You will not experience real freedom unless you spend time learning truth from God's Word. Without this revelation of truth in your life, you will be trapped by falsehoods that will hold you prisoner to the very things from which Jesus desires to set you free.

Bible study should be done consistently. More than on Sunday mornings, the Bible should be a regular part of your reading. Read through it, chapters at a time. Read it in depth, spending time with small sections or short chapters. Read for an overall sense of the book, and study for deeper knowledge. Read it instead of the devotional book or with the devotional book. Read it, and then pick up the book about it. There is no substitute for reading His Word.

Reading the Bible should be done systematically. Follow a reading plan, or devise one yourself. Reading or studying through a book of the Bible gives you a sense of the entire counsel of God's Word. If you only read your favorite parts, you tend to only reinforce what you already know and are not challenged to deal with those truths that are uncomfortable or that do not support your preconceived notions.

Deep understanding isn't required to become a believer, but it is required of those who are believers. Sometimes we emphasize the false idea that a person must know a lot of theology to become a Christian. The plain truth of Scripture is that all you need to know is that you have sinned and that God has provided a remedy for that sin in the person and work of Jesus Christ. Some people, after maturing in their understanding of truth, think, *I had no idea what I was doing when I was baptized. I didn't understand the meaning of my sin or the depth of God's forgiveness. I must not have been saved. I need to do it again.* While no one should be talked out of a deeper commitment to Christ, newfound knowledge does not negate childlike faith at the moment of salvation. Most of those who are married would say some of the same things about love and marriage: "We had no idea what it really meant when we exchanged vows at the altar. We didn't understand the depth of commitment or patience required for marriage." Immature ignorance about love and commitment does not mean a marriage was not valid.

True freedom also comes through an experiential knowledge of Jesus Christ. The word used for "know" in verse 32 implies an experiential knowledge or "coming to know or understand." This means that you cannot be set free by merely sitting in a class or going to a seminar. You are not set free by merely knowing a set of facts about Jesus. You must follow Him on a consistent basis, which means to learn from Him by obeying Him and doing.

This "experienced knowledge" of Him is found only through time and relationship. As you are obedient to Him, you experience His work in your life and come to understand His power and faithfulness. Many people can recite the facts of Jesus's life and even quote His commands, but that doesn't mean that they each have relationship with Him or have been set free. It is through obedience to Him that you exhibit your own faithfulness to Him. As you are faithful to Him, you have the privilege of experiencing His faithfulness. In turn, you are more inclined to trust Him and trust His Word. As you trust Him and exhibit your own faithfulness toward Him, you begin to experience the freedom of the gospel.

Christian growth is a lifelong process. Don't try to take shortcuts. Be patient and persevere. You won't know it all tomorrow, but as you are faithful to grow and study each day, week, and month, at the end of a year you will be farther along than you are now. Commit yourself to the process of growth toward true freedom.

Prayer and Notes

_____

_____

_____

_____

_____

자유

DAY 3

You Are Set Free

And you will know the truth, and the truth will
set you free. (John 8:32)

There are three ways to think about salvation. 1) Justification
speaks to the moment you were saved. At that moment, when
you were justified, you were forgiven of all of your sin by the
blood of Jesus shed on the cross and God looked at you as though
you had no sin. 2) Sanctification is the process of you being saved
as you live on this earth. Already justified, your life is being
molded into the very image of Christ. 3) Glorification is the
moment you will be saved as you leave this earth to be with God
for eternity. You will enter into the very presence of God and He
will bring to completion the work that began at the moment you
were saved.

In this moment of salvation, you were set free. But here, in verse
32 of John 8, Jesus is speaking about the process of being set free.
Jesus uses the future tense saying, "the truth will set you free." He
is describing something different than the moment of salvation,
He is talking about the process of spiritual growth in which you
come to understand your new identity and you learn to live in
freedom.

Freedom grows in you as you grow spiritually. Your knowledge gained through reading the Bible combines with your experience of God's faithfulness and you step toward the experience of freedom. You allow Him to live His life through you and you experience His freedom. This is a lifelong process of spiritual growth and understanding.

You will learn that you are not limited to what others see in you or how you see yourself. You are not a prisoner to the way of life handed down by your ancestors or even that which you have adopted from your peers. You don't have to live in rebellion, finding your identity in who you are not. You are not the sum total of the expectations of your parents, coaches or bosses. You are free!

Understanding the breadth of freedom will be a life long pursuit for you. We will talk more about this in the following days.

Unfortunately, the gift of this freedom and the pursuit of this freedom are not automatic. Even after accepting God's gift of life and forgiveness, there is a struggle and a battle to live in freedom. This spiritual battle is why you must commit to being involved in the process of personal spiritual growth. God will work in you today to prepare you for the battle to come in six months. Allow Him to work through His Word in your life to get your spiritual life where it needs to be next year.

Prayer and Notes

_____

_____

_____

_____

_____

2|6|21

DAY 4

Overcome the Barriers

"But we are descendants of Abraham," they said. "We have never been slaves to anyone. What do you mean, 'You will be set free'?" (John 8:33)

The greatest barrier to freedom is thinking you don't need it or that you already have it apart from Christ. When the other non-believing Jews respond to Jesus they reflect what many think as they come to Christ. Three phrases in their statement in John 8:33 reveal great barriers to the experience of true freedom.

"We are descendants of Abraham" - The Jews who spoke to Jesus claimed a heritage that did not require outside intervention. They saw themselves through the lens of long ago ancestors, not just their immediate parents. They traced their heritage back to Abraham! For these Jews, this heritage was their identity and there was neither way nor reason to deny it. Proud of their ancestry, they were unwilling to accept the freedom offered by Jesus.

Sometimes you can be so caught up in your family identity, who your parents are and how important they are or how important that makes you, that you deny the opportunity to follow Jesus wherever He leads. More than one person has wrecked their own spiritual opportunities because they were intent on protecting their family name or station in life. More than one church has been wrecked by a family or individual who is trying to hold on to an inherited position in the church and community. I am not saying that you should disavow your family, but certainly you should not choose anything over the clear call of Christ. Several times Jesus challenged His followers to do that very thing (Matthew 4:21-22; 8:21-22; 19:28-29; Mark 1:19-20; 10:28-30; Luke 9:59-60; 14:26). Jesus's promise of freedom is powerful because He opens the door for you to break free from the hold of generations.

"We have never been enslaved to anyone." - The Jews make a claim that on its face is preposterous. The most important festival of the Jewish calendar is Passover, a celebration of God's deliverance of the nation from Egyptian slavery. The northern kingdom of Israel disappeared during Assyrian slavery. The Babylonians took the southern kingdom into slavery for 70 years. As they spoke the nation of Israel was under the thumb of the Romans, subject to their laws, and the whims of their governors.

There is deceitfulness in denial that leaves you with a false view of your own circumstance. Most teenagers claim a deep need to not be stereotyped, to be treated as individuals, yet they dress, talk, and think just like their peers. They may reject their parents, but they will conform to a group in school and defying that group is deemed social suicide. Adults bend under the same pressures adapting to a work culture or a social setting to "fit in." This is one reason that advertising works so well. There is a deep hunger to be an individual, but to not stand out too much. The worst kind of bondage is when a prisoner thinks himself to be free, yet he is a slave.

"How can you say 'You will become free'?" - The Jews utter the frustration so many voice: "I can't change." The sense of helplessness you feel, trapped in your life with no way out. Often I've heard people say things like this: "This is just how I am." "I can't help it." "I don't know why I do it." "I've always been like this." The trap of believing that your past must be your future keeps many from walking through the process of being set free, even though they may have made a decision to follow Christ.

One of the great tragedies of this generation is that so many have fallen for the lie that a genetic predisposition means there are no options in life. That is to say, too many think because "you are born this way" you must live "this way." It's easy to understand why you might believe that a lifestyle, life choices, and values that have been ingrained for so many years could never be abandoned or transformed. This is part of what makes the claim of Jesus so amazing. How could He promise freedom from something so deeply ingrained in your identity?

Do you feel caught in one of these traps? Have you allowed your history to dictate your future instead of grabbing the future God has for you? Are you denying that you even need God's help? Have you been caught in the trap of thinking that you can't change? Do you want to change? Do you want to live in God's freedom?

Prayer and Notes

_____

_____

_____

_____

_____

_2/25/21_

DAY 5

You Are Family

> Jesus replied, "I tell you the truth, everyone who sins is a slave of sin. A slave is not a permanent member of the family, but a son is part of the family forever. So if the Son sets you free, you are truly free." (John 8:34-36)

Jesus brings truth serum to challenge self-deception and to deliver you from your bondage. The reality, Jesus says, is that everyone _contradicts point of next paragraph_ who commits sin (which means all of us since we are all sinners) is a slave or in bondage to sin. It doesn't matter who your parents are or how far back you may trace your spiritual lineage, you are responsible for your own life and your own sin. You have no righteous insulation from sin because your parents were good people or because Abraham is your ancestor.

The act of committing sin reveals that the one doing the act is under the power and authority of sin. The word "commits" is a present tense verb. In Greek, the written language of the New Testament, a present tense verb describes current and continual action. It could be translated, "keeps on committing." Jesus is describing a person who continues to commit sin without regret or repentance. The Pharisees thought themselves to be free, but they were in spiritual bondage to sin.

When you are in bondage to sin you are living under the influence of your rebellious human nature. Your worldview is affected by human intuition apart from the truth of God. Your way of responding to the world is determined by selfish motives, not by the fruit of the Spirit. Your reaction to crisis situations and conflict is defensive and focused on self-preservation instead of with godly wisdom and humility. When you are in bondage to sin you don't realize you are held prisoner. You act as everyone around you acts. You respond based on the advice of your peers. Your actions are accepted and endorsed by others because all are in slavery to sin, so everyone around you is living the same way.

But this is not the condition of the believer. Jesus delivers you from sin and by His truth He sets you free from the slavery of sin. In verse 35 Jesus presents the opportunity to become a child of God as opposed to living as a slave to sin.

Jesus sets you free by changing your identity. This change of identity is monumental. You do not have to remain as a slave to sin; you become a child of God!

As a child of God, you are no longer under the sole influence of your rebellious human nature. You are free to resist sin and to cling to truth, integrity, and joy. Your worldview is transformed as you begin seeing the world through His eyes. The fruit of the Spirit works outward in your life and you respond to the world differently. You react to conflict with grace and patience, exhibiting wisdom and humility, knowing that God is in control of your life. You don't worry about being rejected by your peers if you don't act like them because you know you have been fully accepted by God through Christ. You don't have to protect your reputation or save face by conforming to the world because you are secure in your place with Christ.

Your history doesn't have to be altered or hidden. It is what it is and it is forgiven. You are free from your history. Rahab was a prostitute but now is forgiven. Thomas doubted but now is with Jesus. The thief deserved death but now has life eternal.

"Therefore if the Son sets you free, you really will be free." John 8:36

This freedom is not circumstantial, based on what you have done. It is not based on your actions or your inherent value or worth to God. This freedom is based completely on the grace of God on your behalf in sending His Son to the cross.

Once again you see the moment and the process in this verse. Jesus Christ sets you free – this is the moment you receive by faith His forgiveness offered through grace. Then you really will be free – through this process you come to understand and live in freedom. This is justification and sanctification. You need to be set free, that is to be made a child of God so that you can become free, experience knowing Jesus in all His glory.

Freedom from sin, darkness, ignorance, superstition, good and bad expectations, past mistakes, wrong thinking can only be known after Jesus sets you free. This freedom can only be experienced by spending time with God's Word, worshipping Him, praying with Him and following Jesus day after day, year after year.

As you commit yourself to the process of being set free, you come to understand that your identity doesn't have to come from where you were born, what family you come from, who your friends are, your past failures or others expectations. Your identity comes from the work of God on your behalf. You are His child and you are free.

There is a new way to live, a new way to see yourself and a new path to walk. You are free. This is who you are. So live free.

Prayer and Notes

_____

_____

_____

_____

_____

DAY 6

What Were You?

Once you were dead because of your disobedience
and your many sins. (Ephesians 2:1)

Warning: we are going to spend a few days getting depressed
together. Don't worry, there is a point to it, but we have to go
through this to get to the other side.

Have you ever seen the show called, "Who do you think you
are?" It has been on the networks and more recently on TLC. On
the show they take celebrities through an in-depth look at their
ancestry, revealing where they came from and usually a nice story
about someone a few generations before them.

Have you ever done that? Has anyone in your family ever done a
study of your ancestry? There are websites that specialize in helping
people discover their roots. One of the most popular is ancestry.
com which in one year recorded earnings of over $500,000,000.
People search their ancestry, wanting to know where they came
from. Maybe it makes a difference, I don't know. The first Bracewell
in my family to come over from England was an Anglican priest
who spent some time leading a church in Virginia in the 1600's

(the spelling evolved over time and as subsequent generations moved south).

While you may spend time researching your personal history, your individual ancestry, we do share a common heritage. This heritage is not one to be bragged about. We all come from a common place. We have a history among us that certainly is common to us all. It is important to know about that, to examine it and be aware of it, because it helps you understand where you came from, to keep you humble, and to appreciate the magnitude of what God has done for those who put their faith in Him.

Ephesians chapter 2 gives a clear picture of our common heritage. As Paul begins this chapter he gives an honest, brutal assessment of what your life is like without Jesus Christ.

Paul says that you were "dead in your trespasses and sins." Spiritual death is what he is describing here, not physical death. The first thing you see is that spiritual death is very real. Paul is not using a metaphor to describe your life before Christ. He is talking about reality. You were dead in your trespasses and sins. It is interesting that he uses the word "in." He doesn't say, "because of" your trespasses and sins. You are in the middle of your trespasses and sins and you are spiritually dead. There is no spiritual life there. That means that you sin because you are a sinner.

You might think about it this way. When you go to a funeral you see the body in the casket. You may not know everything about how the person died or what factors led to their death, but you do know one thing: they are not going to get up out of that casket during the funeral. They cannot see. They cannot taste. They cannot smell. They cannot do anything. The person is dead. You understand physical death so let's think about spiritual death. A spiritually dead person has no ability to sense things spiritually.

None. You may like to think that you aren't "too" dead, that maybe you can sense some things. But the word is clear here. Paul says that without Christ you are dead in your sins. You have no ability to rescue yourself, to get yourself up out of your situation. You are dead. If Paul wanted to say something less he could have. He could have phrased it as a metaphor, "It was like you were dead …" But that is not what he did. He says you were "dead in your trespasses and sins." This is a very real death. Without Christ, that is your condition.

So consider this: You should not give yourself too much credit for the good you did before you were saved because you were spiritually dead. If you don't get credit for the good stuff you did before you were saved, you also shouldn't get much credit for the good stuff done after salvation. At your very best, before you knew Christ, you were still dead in your trespasses and sins. On your best day, without Christ, you are still dead in your sins, spiritually dead; and God still loved you enough to send His Son for you.

Prayer and Notes

_____

_____

_____

_____

_____

3|7|21

DAY 7

What Have You Done?

in which you previously walked according to the
ways of this world, according to the ruler who
exercises authority over the lower heavens, the
spirit now working in the disobedient.
(Ephesians 2:2)

In the Ephesians 2:2 Paul says this: "you used to live in sin." Not only
is spiritual death very real, but spiritual death overwhelms you.

First: you lived "just like the rest of the world." He is describing
here society, the culture around you. This world is without God
and pulls you away from God. Humanity's attempts to explain
God, explain the existence of the world and how things work in
it, do nothing but hide God from you. It is easier to see this if you
became a believer as an older youth or adult than if you came to
faith when you were a child. Even then, you may not realize how
overwhelmed your life has become by the culture in which you
live. You don't realize how immune you get to things in the world.
Society leaves a callous on your heart and mind to the point where
you no longer are offended by vulgarity or pornography. You can
live in the world and no longer recognize what righteousness
looks like.

Not only does society overwhelm you, Paul goes on to say that you are living according to the ruler of this world. Here he describes the role Satan has in dominating the spiritually dead. In 2 Corinthians 4 Paul says the god of this world has blinded the eyes of those who are without Christ. When you are without Christ, Satan has so much power over your life you don't even realize it. He dominates the world of the spiritually dead. You don't realize that your vision is limited, but it is true. The fact that you don't know it doesn't mean it isn't true. He is the father of lies and you are the believer of lies. Things he tells you about yourself, you believe. When he says that God doesn't love you, you believe it. You are overwhelmed by him.

It is not just the culture, and not just Satan, but look at the end of verse 2. "walk according to the spirit now working in the disobedient." Note that the word "spirit" is not capitalized. He is not talking about some evil spirit but the nature that resides within you. This sin nature within you, in the KJV the word is translated "flesh," wants you to sin. Why do you sin? You sin because you are a sinner. It is your nature. It is what you do. It is your own attempt to bypass God. You want to maneuver away, to escape His will and His commands. Even as a believer there is a struggle, but before Christ it isn't a struggle, it is the way you live. It's the way everyone around you lives so it seems pretty normal. It doesn't seem odd at all. From the world's perspective, the weird ones are those Christians who don't live like everyone else. 1 Peter 4:4 says this: "Of course, your former friends are surprised when you no longer plunge into the flood of wild and destructive things they do. So they slander you." (NLT) In the world of today, do not be surprised when others look at a believer trying to live a faithful life and think him to be odd. You are peculiar. You stand out. Everyone else lives one way because they don't know anything different.

When you are in a culture where Christianity is not the prime cultural identity, you will see how odd evangelical Christianity looks to the general population. In so many places in the world the culture has moved so far from Christian ideals that those who attempt to honor God with their lives stand against almost everything others take as normal. Living a Christ-honoring life is truly counter-cultural. Christianity is the only true counter-cultural movement in the history of the world.

Prayer and Notes

_____

_____

_____

_____

_____

DAY 8

3/31/21

Who Were You?

> We too all previously lived among them in our
> fleshly desires, carrying out the inclinations of
> our flesh and thoughts, and we were by nature
> children under wrath as the others were also.
> (Ephesians 2:3)

Spiritual death is very real, overwhelming and is universal. Paul says it is not just about them, but about all. In verse 3 he changes pronouns from "you" to "we." Here he includes himself: "We too all lived among them in our spiritual death." We were all spiritually dead. So you can't read this passage and think only about the poor ones who don't have the good fortune to be you. This is our common heritage. No matter where you came from or who your parents and grandparents were, we all share this condition. This is who we all were. You didn't know God. You didn't have a heart for God. You weren't searching for God before God came to search for you. You wouldn't have sought out Jesus. You were spiritually dead. Left to yourself, you would live and die in the midst of your sin.

This was your nature. You lived this way. This is how your life went. It was just what you did. Even your thoughts, your reason, and your logic were completely impaired by sin. You couldn't think straight. Romans 12:2 Paul says: "Do not be conformed to this world but be transformed by the renewing of your mind." J.B. Philips has a great translation of this verse: "Do not let the world squeeze you into its mold." That is what happens isn't it? The world just squeezes you into the same mold, where everyone thinks and acts alike. Instead, you must be transformed. It is not just what you do but also what you think. Your thoughts are completely overwhelmed by spiritual death.

Spiritual death dooms you. In the next part of the verse Paul says that "we were by nature under wrath." Do you realize that the danger for a person who is spiritually dead is not from Satan but from God? The wrath you should fear is God's wrath. Satan has done what he can do. You need to be in fear of God's wrath.

Paul adds in verse 12 that the Gentiles were utterly hopeless. Without Christ, you are utterly hopeless. You are dead in your sins. You are dead in your trespasses. You have no hope. Consider this, if you are without God, to whom will you call? To whom will you cry out if He is not your God? Who will you beseech to rescue you, if He is not your God? You have no one to call. Utterly hopeless.

If the passage ended there, this would be the most depressing chapter every written, but that is not all the story.

Verse 3 of chapter 2 is followed by verse 4. It begins with two of the greatest words in all of Scripture. These two words may form the most important phrase in the history of the world, "But God." You were dead in your trespasses and sins, you had no hope and nothing to claim spiritually, "but God." Paul didn't leave the story without a proper ending.

Prayer and Notes

_____

_____

_____

_____

_____

4/1/2021

DAY 9

You Are Alive

> But God, who is rich in mercy, because of His great love that He had for us, made us alive with the Messiah even though we were dead in trespasses. You are saved by grace! Together with Christ Jesus He also raised us up and seated us in the heavens, so that in the coming ages He might display the immeasurable riches of His grace through His kindness to us in Christ Jesus. (Ephesians 2:4-7)

Who is this God who came to you while you were dead in your trespasses and sins? He is a God rich in mercy, one who has great love. In verse 7 He says He will display the immeasurable riches of His love ..."

This God is rich in mercy and has great love for you. He will display the riches of His glorious grace in His kindness towards you. That's who this God is. You cannot be rich in mercy and love unless you do something. You can be rich in words about mercy and love and do nothing. If you are truly rich in mercy and love, then you must act it out. What did He do? He sent His Son Christ to pay the penalty of our sin and then also to make you alive (v. 4).

Where were you? You were dead. You were spiritually dead. You had no spiritual life or abilities whatsoever and then God made you alive. Even though you were dead, He made you alive.

In verse 6 Paul says that God raised you up with Christ and seated you in the heavens. If you are a believer, you have placed your faith in Christ, then you are no longer dead in your trespasses and sins. You are no longer overwhelmed by spiritual death. You are no longer without choice or ability. You are no longer a person who cannot see the way out of sin and temptation. You are no longer a person who sees only the way of the world. You are now alive. You've been raised up and seated in the heavens with Christ. You have been saved from all of this.

That's why he says in verse 8 and 9 that you are saved by grace, not by your works so that none can boast. Do you see how these verses fit into the whole passage of Ephesians 2? You are saved by grace. God loved you so much that He saved you even though you didn't deserve it. You were dead. God didn't save you because you were so wonderful that He just had to have you on His side. You were dead in your sins. You were without worth and with no spiritual value whatsoever. But God loved you. He made you alive. He raised you up and He seated you with Him. He saved you by His grace. He loved you so much He wanted you in spite of your sin.

So you should be humble. You know that all you are spiritually is fully because of Him. You are saved by His grace, not by your works. So don't brag or boast. You are not saved by your works; so why would you think that your works would keep you saved? All that you are is because of Him. Look at the verbs. They show that He was acting and you were receiving. Look at all that God has done for you.

So you worship Him. You praise His name. He redeemed you from your ancestry, our common beginning. This should swell up songs of praise from you as you look at who you were and who He made you to be. Sometimes you can fall into the trap of thinking that you were pretty good to begin with. You can dismiss thoughts of your own previous sin, thinking that God is lucky to have you. Don't fall into this trap. Without God, you are nothing and have nothing.

When you look at others, don't consider their sin without remembering that you were once dead in your trespasses and sins without Christ. Love them as Christ loves them. It's easy to be judgmental and see all those other "poor lost folks." Remember, those whose sin is appalling to you are simply dead in their trespasses and sins. They know no other way to live. Remember that you were there once also. Love them. Find some way to love them.

Prayer and Notes

_____

_____

_____

_____

_____

DAY 10

You Are Righteous

> Therefore, since we have been declared righteous by faith, we have peace with God through our Lord Jesus Christ. (Romans 5:1)

What is it that makes a good Christian? When you say, "You need to act like a Christian." What does that mean? Is it the way you dress, movies you go see, music you listen to or don't listen to, places you can go, words you can or can't say? What is it that makes a good Christian?

We have a lot of ideas about what makes a good Christian and most of the time we are focused on superficial things. We look at what we can see and make judgments or recommendations based on what we can see. The problem is that when you judge based on what you can see, once you have changed what can be seen transformation usually ceases. Then the things that really need to be addressed in your life are never addressed. A person says, "Now that I look like a Christian and act like a Christian there is nothing left to do." At this point, the spiritual life becomes stagnant.

But what does the scripture say about being a Christian, about what defines a "good Christian"?

Chapter 5 of Romans begins with "Therefore." Because of all that has been said to this point, that we are all sinners and are saved only through faith in the life, death, and resurrection of Jesus Christ, we are now "declared righteous by faith."

Twice in these verses Paul uses the phrase, "by faith." Faith changes everything. Hear that again, "Faith changes everything." Before faith, you are the sum total of what you have done. Everything in life is because of you. What were you? You were helpless, a sinner, the enemy of God, dead in your trespasses and sin, hopeless, without God, without faith, without Christ, and without life. You had nothing.

Look at the immediate change that happens by faith. In verse 1 he says that you are "declared righteous" by faith. Have you ever noticed this phrase, "declared righteous" or "made righteous"? By your faith in Christ, you are declared righteous. This is extremely important. This is at the center of what it means to be Christian. It's not about what clothes you wear or what songs you sing or what movies you watch. Those things are not at the center of what it means to be Christian. When you put your faith in Christ you are declared righteous. God looks at you and says, "I declare you to be righteous." Not by your works or by your innate goodness, it is God's declaration because of your faith.

What does the word righteous mean? Without fault. Holy. Pure. Completely forgiven. Free from any and all accusation. Think back to everything you have done. The moment you accept Jesus Christ as Savior, He declares you righteous. He doesn't say this to you: "Now that you've declared me your Savior, if you'll start doing some good things then I'll start forgiving some of the bad things. The more good you do, the more of the bad I'll forget." That is not what happens. The scripture says that at the moment you put your faith in Jesus Christ you are at that moment, by the only, holy judge of the universe, declared righteous. Everything in your past is gone. It is all forgiven and removed from your account. You may not have forgiven yourself or forgotten it, but God has declared you righteous. You are now holy. You are forgiven. You are free. God will not listen to any accusation made against you. You are declared righteous.

Many spend the entirety of their Christian lives trying to work their way out of previous trouble. They make multiple efforts to somehow earn God's favor, to relieve Him of the heartache caused by previous actions. This is an incorrect view of what happens at salvation. If you believe God's Word, then you must take it honestly for what it says, speaking truth to your life. You are declared righteous by your faith. He says it again in verse 9: "since we have now been declared righteous by His blood." By faith in the cross, you are declared righteous. Nothing will be remembered against you. This is why it's called "Good News."

All other religions teach that you must work your way out of trouble. They tell you to make the balance sheet of your good works and your sins tip in favor of the good. Some, even after becoming Christians, still live this way. The scripture is clear. God doesn't love you more because you've done good stuff. He loved you when you were a sinner as much as He'll ever love you. It wasn't when you began to figure things out and get your life in order that He began to love you more. You were in the midst of your sin when Christ died for you. It was when you were His enemy that His love was great on your behalf. Then the moment you accepted His gift and trusted His love, He declared you righteous.

Stephen Brazzel

Prayer and Notes

_____

_____

_____

_____

_____

4|11|2021

DAY 11

You Stand in God's Grace

> We have also obtained access through Him by
> faith into this grace in which we stand, and we
> rejoice in the hope of the glory of God. (Romans 5:2)

In Romans 5:2 Paul continues by saying that not only are you
declared righteous by your faith, but you have also "obtained
access by faith into this grace in which we stand." The second
thing that happens by your faith is that you gain access into His
grace. You get a place where you can stand in the middle of the
grace of God. This means that you can enter into His presence,
into His throne room. This is not because you have merited access
by your works, but by the grace of God through our faith in
His work on our behalf. You can now enter into the presence of
the King of kings and the Lord of lords every moment of every
day. Not because you are a good Christian, but because He is a
great and loving God. Any time. Any season. You can enjoy the
blessings of God working in your behalf.

Grace is a blessing. It is God working on your behalf. Some
describe grace as the unmerited favor of God. Sometimes you
focus on grace only in salvation, but God's grace abounds to you
throughout your life as a believer. Grace is God working on your

behalf, in your life, through your life, for the benefit of your life because He wants to.

By faith, you obtain access into that grace in which you stand. To stand in the grace of God is to reside there, to live there. As a believer, you can live in the grace of God. You can take up residence there. You don't merely get to visit His grace every few days or weeks. You can live there. Enjoy His work on your behalf always. Not because you are so good, but by faith. Faith changes everything.

This is another phrase found repeatedly in this passage that must be addressed. The phrase is: "through Him."

> In verse 1 – "...we have peace through our Lord Jesus Christ."
> Verse 2 – "Through Him, we have obtained access ..."

You were at war with God, you were His enemy (Rom. 5:10). Were you at war with Him because of the terrible things He had done to you? No. You were at war because you had declared war on Him. You knew how to make your own path, how to live your life best. You lived your own life apart from God. You despised His truth and dismissed His commands. And now, by faith, through Him, you are at peace with God. He declared peace.

He made peace by sending the offering. The offering is His Son. Through Jesus Christ, you are at peace with Him. You are no longer at war with Him. You are no longer His enemy.

Do not become obsessed with trying to impress Him. You are already at peace. You do not give your offering or tithe to make peace with God. Your tithe doesn't even help make peace with God. It is only through the blood of Jesus that you can be at peace with Him. Don't try to impress Him. You may spend a lot of your

Christian existence trying to impress God. You don't have to impress Him. He has declared peace.

Through Him, you stand in His grace. You are no longer held to some arbitrary standard that you can never fully meet. You don't have to be frustrated by the Christian life, thinking that if you can ever get all of your life on track then finally God will be happy with you. You do not have to hit the moving target of Christian Cultural Goodness: certain clothes, certain actions, some other church cultural standard no one can live up to. As a believer standing in His grace, you are free. It is by faith that you are in His grace, through His blood.

So do not stand in judgment over someone for how they have not met your standard, whatever it is. Allow God to work on them as He sees fit, instead of trying to impose your own standard on them as you see fit. What is important to you may not be of primary importance to God in someone else's life. You may look at someone and think you know what needs to change, but what if that is not most important to God? What you see, what is important to you, is not always high on God's agenda and may not even be on His agenda. This is true of alcoholism, drug abuse, marital infidelity or homosexuality, any of those considered public sins. These things need to change, but they are not always the first to be changed. Sometimes you can settle for changing what can be seen rather than living in the grace of God and allowing His Spirit to work in the life of a believer to do what must be done first. This is standing in grace. When you stand in grace you know that only by faith will things change. So you can wait, pray and trust God's Spirit to work by His grace to do what He wants done.

Prayer and Notes

_____

_____

_____

_____

_____

DAY 12

You Will Never Be Unloved by God

> And not only that, but we also rejoice in our afflictions, because we know that affliction produces endurance, endurance produces proven character, and proven character produces hope. This hope will not disappoint us, because God's love has been poured out in our hearts through the Holy Spirit who was given to us. (Romans 5:3-5)

All of this is followed by one of the craziest verses in all of scripture, Romans 5:3: " …we also rejoice in our afflictions …" What is wrong with Paul? "We rejoice in our afflictions?" Through Christ, you are no longer hopeless in the face of affliction.

His Spirit fills your life and because of His presence you are now able to rejoice in affliction. You know that this affliction is not the end and is not the determining factor in your life. This affliction will not be the end of your story. Because God has saved you, the Holy Spirit has filled you, and you have been declared righteous through the blood of Jesus. Whatever the hardship you will face, this world is not your last, best hope. You have hope beyond this. If you will be faithful and wait on the Lord (that's called endurance), God will build character in you, and as He builds that character you will discover the hope He has set before you. For this reason, you rejoice. Not because afflictions are fun but because you know these afflictions are not the end.

Through Christ, you are saved from the wrath of God. No longer a sinner, you are declared righteous. You don't have to work to be saved because you can't do it anyway. You can rest in the salvation that comes through faith.

Through Him, you are reconciled. You are brought back into proper relationship with God as He meant it to be in the beginning. You are united with Him.

Don't think you could ever be unloved by God. You might think of this relationship like the relationship between a parent and a child. Nothing that child does will keep the parent from loving him. There may be things that will frustrate or make the parent angry. But there is no way they can do anything that will cause the parent to cease loving. The child may not like what has to be done to show love, but they will always be loved. That love, from a parent to a child, pales in comparison to God's love for you. So great is His love that He gave His only Son to die for you.

Being a good Christian has nothing to do with ritual. Being a good Christian has nothing to do with regulation. Being a Christian is all about relationship. Because you have put your faith in Him, He has declared you righteous. You now stand in His grace. You cannot be taken from His grace. Through Him, you are at peace. Through Him, you have access to His throne every moment of every day of your life. Through Him, you are reconciled. Through Him, you are saved. Through Him, your life is lived by faith.

Don't settle to merely have the outward aspects of your life look like a Christian. You don't follow God because you are afraid of what will happen if you don't. You follow because you've learned to love Him. You want to honor Him. You know you will never be unloved by Him.

Prayer and Notes

_____

_____

_____

_____

_____

DAY 13

You Are Built Up in Christ

> Therefore, as you have received Christ Jesus the
> Lord, walk in Him, rooted and built up in Him
> and established in the faith, just as you were taught,
> overflowing with gratitude. (Colossians 2:6-7)

How is it that you receive Christ as your Lord? Do you meet a
bunch of standards of behavior? Do you check off a list of activities
and then declare yourself to subsequently have Christ as your
Lord? As people of the Word you know, the only way you can
receive Christ as your Lord is by faith. You just have to trust the
Lord to forgive your sins, put your life in His hands, trusting that
what Christ did on the cross was sufficient. By believing in what
He did you put your trust in Him as Lord and Savior.

Paul says, "as you have received Christ Jesus the Lord," (how did
this happen, by *faith*) so "walk in Him." Commonly you can fall
into this trap of receiving Christ by faith and then think you must
meet all the standards to keep Him happy by your walk. You think
that the things you do and don't do, things you say and don't say,
watch and don't watch are the things that keep God happy. But
that is not what scripture says.

One of the impactful things for me has been looking at all the things God has done for me in my life. You see, it is good news for a reason. It is not just good news for salvation, but good news for all of life. So let's look at this passage to see all that God has done. See what God has already done for you.

Rooted and built up in Him, established in the faith. God grows your roots deep into His very being. When you give Him your life you are rooted in Him and nothing can pull you up. It's not because you have done it, it's because He has done it. He has rooted you in Him. This is true no matter when you become a Christian. Whether you are 5, 10, 15 or 55 when you put your faith in Him, He roots you in Himself. You may not live like a firmly rooted believer all the time, but those roots are there. They aren't there because you are such a good person, they are there because He rooted you, He established you.

As you work our way through chapter 2 of Colossians you will see other things that God has done for you: filled by Him (v. 10), circumcised in Him (v. 11), buried with Him (v. 12), raised with Him (v. 12), made alive with Him (v. 13), forgiven (v. 13).

It is because of what God has done in your life that you are then "overflowing with gratitude." You need to consistently be reminded of the things God has done so that you will consistently give thanks to Him. If you begin to look at only today or yesterday and see only the current struggle or crisis, you may forget that God has already acted in great ways in your life. You may then even forget to be thankful, to have an attitude of gratitude.

It is good to begin the practice of regularly listing or reviewing the work of God in your life to keep you in the habit of giving thanks. This is not just for one month of the year but for every month, every week, every day. Start your list today. Add to it tomorrow. What has God done for which you should be thankful?

Prayer and Notes

_____

_____

_____

_____

_____

DAY 14

You Are Filled by Him

> Be careful that no one takes you captive through philosophy and empty deceit based on human tradition, based on the elemental forces of the world, and not based on Christ. For the entire fullness of God's nature dwells bodily in Christ, and you have been filled by Him, who is the head over every ruler and authority. (Colossians 2:8-10)

Paul knew that the believers in Colosse were dealing with a group who wanted to impose the legalism of Judaism on the church. There were also those who brought their own pagan philosophy into the church and tried to impose a syncretism that would meld together Christianity with humanistic philosophy. I think if Paul were writing this verse today he might say this, *"Be careful that no one takes you captive by telling you there are certain things you can do to make yourself a good person instead of trusting in Christ. Be careful that no one takes you captive thinking that there is a way that Christians dress, and there is an official Christian look."*

It's a scary thing when you get the idea that there is a way you must look if you are going to go to church. Sometimes you get so concerned about those outer things, the things you can see, that you force them on people. The tragedy is that you can force a person to look Christian and talk Christian and in so doing you substitute cultural Christianity for spiritual transformation. What's really important to God may not be what they are wearing. It's most likely that what is most important to Him is a heart issue that you cannot see and you cannot change. But sometimes you substitute these outer changes for the real transformation that needs to take place.

Any philosophical construct or life change recommendation that is not based on Christ is less than the gospel. Don't settle for anything less than the gospel.

Colossians 2:9 is one of the greatest statements about the deity of Christ. Some people argue that Jesus was a great man but not God and that there are no claims that He was God. Those people haven't read Colossians 2:9. The entire fullness of God dwelled in Him. He is God in the flesh. 100% God. 100% man. He is completely God and still is. The verse uses a present tense verb "dwells" not a past tense. He still is God.

We often stop at verse 9 because of the significant theology, but we should not miss the power of verse 10. "You have been filled by Him." Another way to translate that phrase is "have been made complete." What does that mean? You "will be filled?" No. You "have been filled." This is a past perfect. It means, something happened and continues to have an effect forever. How did you receive Christ? By faith. What else happened? You were filled and remain filled by the holy God of the universe. You have been made complete.

You may think you need to work up the Christian scale or the religious scale. When you accepted Christ you were made complete by Him. You were filled by Him. You received all of Him. You didn't get just a portion and then as you work yourself farther into His good graces you will receive the rest. NO. You received all of Him. He filled you. He came into your life. You have all of God in you. You were made complete. You have everything you will ever need to live your life as a believer right now. You are complete.

His presence may not always show out in your life, but do not think it is not there. It's not there because you feel like it's there. It's not there because you had an emotional experience and now you have it. It's there because you placed your trust in Christ and He acted in your life to fill you by the power of the Holy Spirit.

You can go down to the coastline of the Mediterranean Sea with a large glass and dip that glass under the surface of the water and fill that glass with the most beautiful clear blue water. When you pull that glass up from the water you will notice that there is a lot of water not in your glass, but your glass is full of the Mediterranean Sea. When you accept Christ as your Lord and Savior, all of you is filled up with Him. Everything He is now fills your life. God still exists outside of your life, but your life is completely full of all that He is.

Prayer and Notes

_____

_____

_____

_____

_____

5/16/2021

DAY 15

You Were Raised With Him

> You were also circumcised in Him with a circumcision not done with hands, by putting off the body of flesh, in the circumcision of the Messiah. Having been buried with Him in baptism, you were also raised with Him through faith in the working of God, who raised Him from the dead. (Colossians 2:11-12)

In Colossians 2:11 Paul isn't talking about fleshly circumcision but the spiritual cutting away of the sinful nature that destroys your life. In Corinthians he says this nature has been put away or buried as you would bury something that has died. In verse 12 he says, "having been buried … you were raised."

Notice the verb forms. He says you "were circumcised … having been buried … you were raised." All of these things occur at the moment of salvation when you give your life to Christ. He cuts away this old self; it has no power over you. Now sometimes you let it rise back up and influence your life, but it has no power over you. You may feel like the old self has power, but feelings do not make it so. You have been filled with Him. You are complete with Him. That old self was cut away. You have been buried with Him. You have been raised with Him. These things happened at salvation. Those old ways of thinking, acting, believing have been removed and you have been raised up to a new life. So as you were saved, now walk in Him.

Don't live as a person who is trying to conquer the sinful nature, but as one who had it cut away and has now been raised to live a different life. You are not held by that old nature anymore. You have freedom from it. One of the things I discovered in the book of Psalms was how David talked about the people who were trying to pull him back into sin. Those people were not looking out for David's best interests. They didn't want him to do well. They didn't care about David at all. They were purposely trying to destroy him.

Sin looks good and so draws you in. It looks appealing and profitable. But those who are luring you into greed, pornography, bitterness, alcoholism, are not looking out for your good. They are trying to destroy your life. They are purposely deceiving you.

If you have "friends" who are pulling you back into that life, then you need to understand something. They are not pulling you back because they think it will be good for you; they are pulling you back because it will be good for them. They want you to validate their sin by enticing you to walk away from your Lord. They want to feel better about their deception because misery loves company. Sin pulls you hard.

But you aren't that person any longer. You are free. Freedom means you don't have to fall into that. You are not held by that. You have been raised by Him and now you have a different kind of life. This life is not different because you want to check off the boxes and make God happy but because He lives in you, has filled you, and given you the ability to make different choices. His Spirit in you allows you to see the world differently, to understand it from His perspective and to choose to be obedient out of joy, not an obligation.

Prayer and Notes

_____

_____

_____

_____

_____

DAY 16

You Are Forgiven

> And when you were dead in trespasses and in the uncircumcision of your flesh, He made you alive with Him and forgave us all our trespasses. (Colossians 2:13)

This passage takes us back to the beginning of Ephesians 2. It can be very depressing until you realize that all the verbs are past tense. "You were dead." As a quick reminder, Paul isn't saying it was like you were dead, but you were dead. That is in your past, but now you are alive. He made you alive. He completed you. He filled you. He cut off the sinful nature. He buried it. He raised you. He made you alive. He forgave your trespasses.

One of the hardest things for you to do is accept God's complete forgiveness. Do you remember the verse that says "forgive and forget?" No, you don't because it isn't in the Bible. Do you know why that verse isn't in the Bible? Because God knows you can't forget. But what does God do with our sin? He removes it. He lets it go. He doesn't hold it over your head anymore. He forgives you. You may think of all the bad and rebellious things you have done, even as a believer. You may still remember your sins. God forgives. Will you allow yourself to be forgiven? Will you allow yourself

51

to accept God's forgiveness? Will you allow Him to forgive your drunkenness, your affair, your anger, your bitter words to your family, your pettiness? These are the things He forgives. When you were dead in your trespasses and sins, He made you alive and forgave all your sins.

Did you notice the verb tense of the word "forgave?" It's a past tense verb.

Did you notice the important three letter word in there also? "all"

He doesn't just forgive the sins from the moment you are saved back to your birth, He forgives them all. That means the ones you have committed since that day and the ones you will commit tomorrow and the next day and next year are all forgiven.

Does this really mean "all?" Yes, Christ's death on the cross was sufficient for *all* of your sin. When He died on the cross 2000 years ago, He died for your sin even though you hadn't been born. When you accepted Him as your Lord and Savior by faith, how did He forgive your sin? Did He say, *Oh forget it, no big deal; you are such a good person anyway?* No. You were dead in your trespasses and sin and He forgave you. He forgave you in that situation. He forgave all your trespasses. Take a deep breath and just for a moment realize this: All my sin is forgiven.

That's GOOD NEWS! That's the gospel! All of your sin is forgiven. Stop beating yourself up. Stop holding things over your own head, feeling guilty about them, and stop beating everybody else up. It's FORGIVEN!

Prayer and Notes

_____

_____

_____

_____

_____

5/12/21

DAY 17

Your Battle Has Been Won

> He erased the certificate of debt, with its
> obligations, that was against us and opposed to
> us, and has taken it out of the way by nailing it to
> the cross. He disarmed the rulers and authorities
> and disgraced them publicly; He triumphed over
> them by Him. (Colossians 2:14-15)

There is a certificate of death attached to your life because of your
sin. The list of your sin is there. What did God do? He erased it.
Some think that when you get to heaven there is going to be a long
list of failures pinned to a board. You think your first few hundred
years in eternity will be answering for these sins before God finally
lets you come to the good part of heaven where all the fun is. This
is WRONG! That certificate of death has been erased.
debt

That certificate has obligations. You find the obligations in your
guilt. *I've done this wrong, I need to do some good things to balance
the scales. I will perform for God so that He will see how good I am
and then He won't be so mad at me for the other stuff I've done.*
These obligations are against you. They destroy your life. The
certificate is your enemy. It keeps you from Christ.

But God has taken it out of the way, removing it from your presence. How did He do this? By nailing it to the cross. Do you want to know what happened at the cross? It wasn't just Jesus hanging on that cross, it was all your sin. On that cross, where Jesus was nailed, was the list of your sins. Your certificate of debt was nailed to the cross with Him. Everything you've ever done that disappointed and displeased was nailed to the cross right there with Him.

> He made the One who did not know sin to be sin for us, so that we might become the righteousness of God in Him. (2 Corinthians 5:21)

God reached back with one hand to the beginning of time, to Adam and Eve in the garden, and with the other hand He reached far into your future. He gathered together in His mighty hands every sin that has ever been committed and will ever be committed and He placed those sins on Jesus as He hung on the cross. He made Him who knew no sin to be sin for you that you might be the righteousness of God.

It's important that you understand the usage of the pronouns in this verse 15. God the Father disarmed the rulers and disgraced the rulers publicly. God the Father triumphed over the rulers and authorities by God the Son.

All the sin and trespasses that have held you down and dominated your life have been triumphed over by the Father through the work of the Son on the cross. He cut them off, buried them, raised you up, and made you alive forgiving you of all your sin. That certificate of death that still, sometimes, sits over your head has been removed from you. You are free from its guilt and obligations. You don't have to make God happy. You don't have to perform for Him. You are free. You are forgiven.

So now you can follow God wherever. You don't have to match someone else's expectations. <u>You are free to follow God wherever He might lead</u>. You are His. He made you alive. He forgave you. You are free to follow Him as He leads. Aren't those the songs that you sing? "Wherever He leads I'll go" "I have decided to follow Jesus" You don't sing these songs: "I'll follow the rules" "I'll make everyone else happy"

You can allow God to change you as He decides. You can yield to Him as He wants. The beautiful thing is this: you can do the same for others. They don't have to change to make you happy or comfortable, you can be content to let God work in them and on them as He sees fit. The thing God wants to change in you may very well be something no one can see. And that which He wants to change in someone else may be what you cannot see. Not only that, it will probably be something that only God can change anyway.

The good news is you don't have to hide from God because of your shortcomings. He made you alive. He forgave you. He loves you. He filled you. You are His and you will never be unloved. So don't run from Him and don't hide from Him like Adam and Eve in the garden. Just come to Him. He loves you.

Prayer and Notes

_____

_____

_____

_____

_____

DAY 18

You Are Hidden with Christ

> So if you have been raised with the Messiah, seek what is above, where the Messiah is, seated at the right hand of God. ² Set your minds on what is above, not on what is on the earth. ³ For you have died, and your life is hidden with the Messiah in God. (Colossians 3:1-3)

You must keep in mind that the pagan religions of Paul's day said little to nothing about personal morality. A worshiper could bow before an idol, put his offering on the altar, and go back to live the same old life of sin. What a person believed had no direct relationship with how he behaved and no one would condemn a person for his behavior. But the Christian faith brought a whole new concept into pagan society: what you believe has a very definite connection with how you behave!

As chapter three of Colossians begins Paul is making a move from the theological to the practical. We are going to start making that move with him as we work through these 30 days. Paul begins with a quick review of what has been said earlier in Colossians and he does so by employing a verbal tool that doesn't come across very well in English. He uses the word "if" in verse 1 and you might take this as an added element of uncertainty about what you have already seen. But this usage in the original Greek carries this sense with it: "If you have been raised, which you most certainly have, seek what is above." You could almost put in place of the word "if" the word "since." "Since you have been raised with the Messiah …"

Then he uses three verbs showing completed action – "raised," "died," and "hidden." Each of these verbs indicates a completed action, something that occurred at the moment of salvation. Paul says you are "raised with the Messiah." Your identity is with Christ and His resurrection, not with the world. You are no longer like those who are dead in their sin because you have been raised through the same power that raised Christ from the dead.

You have died. These old desires and ways of life do not have the hold on you they once did, in spite of how you may feel or think you have died to the old life. You are set free through that death to live a life you could never have apart from the work of God in your life.

These first two words you have seen before, but the third one introduces a new idea. Paul says your life is hidden with Christ. To be hidden with Christ implies both concealment and safety. To be hidden away so that the enemy cannot harm you. The enemy has no ability to reach you because you have been hidden with Christ. No matter what others may say about you or try to do to hurt you, your life is safe with Christ.

Being hidden with Christ also implies invisibility and security. This means that your life becomes so completely immersed in the presence of Christ that you are no longer seen by others. Christ is the one who others see when they look at you. This is a place of complete security. Your life is secure with Him; your salvation cannot be lost or misplaced because your life is now hidden with

Christ. Dr. A.T. Robertson, comments on this: "So here you are in Christ who is in God, and no burglar, not even Satan himself, can separate you from the love of God in Christ Jesus (Rom. 8:31-39)"

In this condition, Paul says to do two things continually: seek what is above and set your minds on what is above. These are both present tense verbs meaning they describe continuous action. You could translate them like this: "keep on seeking what is above" and "keep on setting your mind on what is above." You should constantly keep your affections and attention fixed on the things of heaven and eternity. There should be urgency about how you set your attention.

How do you understand what Paul means by the phrase "what is above"? Paul isn't advocating withdrawal from the world, but a proper perspective on the world and its accolades. Glory is your destiny so those things that will persist in glory should be your aim while here on earth. What will persist in glory? Primarily, people. It's not that you shouldn't earn money or try to build great things, but remember that the only people will last for eternity. Don't steamroll over people to build something that will be gone in a few years.

Prayer and Notes

_____

_____

_____

_____

_____

5/19/2024

DAY 19

You Live a Different Life

Therefore, put to death what belongs to your worldly nature: sexual immorality, impurity, lust, evil desire, and greed, which is idolatry. Because of these, God's wrath comes on the disobedient and you once walked in these things when you were living in them. But now you must also put away all the following: anger, wrath, malice, slander, and filthy language from your mouth. Do not lie to one another, since you have put off the old self with its practices (Colossians 3:5-9)

It has been firmly established that you don't live to please God so that He won't destroy you or judge you. The cross has removed all the wrath of God from your life so that now you are free and able to live in relationship to Him. Your relationship with Him is not based on fear of retribution or fear of punishment but is based on honor, respect, and gratitude.

Often a young child will obey parents out of an innate desire to make them happy, to please the parent. As they get to middle elementary, or even a teenager, they will obey parents out of the fear of what will happen if they don't. The parent might not choose this motivation, but few parents will turn down something that works to keep their child out of trouble.

Hopefully, as the child grows and matures, the child moves from being afraid of the parents to understanding that the parent has the best interests of the child in mind. The child will begin to respond to the love of the parent by respecting and wanting to honor the parent. Out of genuine gratitude, he will seek out and listen to the wisdom of the parent. She will earnestly want parental input into how to make good, wise decisions. These are some of the best days of parenthood.

Your desire to please God comes from the same place of growth and maturity. Early on you may be trying to please God, to make Him happy, but then you might move to just trying to keep Him off of your back. You need to move to the place of honor and gratitude, realizing that He has made it possible for you to live a different life than before. He has set you free, raised you up, and forgiven you.

So put to death the things of this world pulling you away from God. Change your life course.

Paul is specific in Colossians as he names some of the traps of this world leading you away from God. This is not unusual as Paul often makes lists of things to walk away from several times in his letters. This list is divided into two that could be described in this way: the sins of personal satisfaction and the sins in good standing.

The sins of personal satisfaction are those that come from a desire to distort and pervert the good things designed by God.

Sexual immorality is any sex outside the bond of marriage. Pornography is the largest growth industry on the internet. It grosses more each year in the U.S. than all pro sports combined. It distorts the God created nature of relationships between husbands and wives.

Impurity is a defilement associated with sexual immorality and describes those things resulting from the influence of a sexually immoral lifestyle. Lust is the misdirected fulfillment of natural bodily appetites. It is most often associated with sex but can be about material things.

Evil desires are uncontrolled passions and habitual lost. Greed is longing for something that belongs to someone else and longing for something that is outside of God's will for your life.

The next list is called the "sins in good standing" because you are so accustomed to anger, critical attitudes, lying, and coarse humor among believers that you are no longer upset or convicted about these sins. You would be shocked to see a church member commit some sensual sin, but you will watch him lose his temper in a church business meeting and think nothing of it.

Anger is an unholy dissatisfaction with someone else. There is righteous indignation that is not sin, but most often you don't meet the high standard of righteous anger. Rage is uncontrolled anger, a quick temper. Malice is misdirected anger. Malice plans and executes evil and rejoices at the failures of those who are hated.

Slander is hateful speech that defames character. Filthy language is obscene speech. The bar for this has moved lower and lower in culture as people will now say things in public that would never have been said just a couple of decades ago. Lying is the ultimate violation of trust in any relationship.

You must confront these deeds in your life and put them away. Because of the work of Christ in your life and the presence of the Holy Spirit, you now have the power and freedom to live differently. Look at the list. Are you convicted by the Holy Spirit?

Prayer and Notes

_____

_____

_____

_____

_____

DAY 20

You Have a New Self

> and have put on the new self. You are being renewed in knowledge according to the image of your Creator. In Christ there is not Greek and Jew, circumcision and uncircumcision, barbarian, Scythian, slave and free; but Christ is all and in all. (Colossians 3:10-11)

The good news is that the putting off of the old self, the battle against the flesh, is not merely a battle of self-will over sin. The old self has been put off through the work of God in your life and He has raised you up as a new creation (2 Corinthians 5:17).

In these verses Paul says renewal is taking place in your life. The phrase he uses is interesting because it is a present tense passive verb translated here, "you are being renewed." This means that a constant renewal is taking place in your life and it is being done to you, not by you. Look carefully, "you are being renewed." This means that someone is acting on your life to renew your life. God Himself is the actor here. Since it is a present tense verb it means that He keeps on renewing your life. He is continually refreshing your life to be continuously victorious over sin.

The model He is using as a guide for your renewal is Himself, "the image of your Creator." He is working to renew your life so that you might live as you were created to live. Through the death and resurrection of Christ, God is now working to get you back to what He originally created you to be. He is restoring you to the original plan.

Sin is not your old self rising up, because it has been crucified, put off. Sin happens because of the imperfect process of growth in the new self. You are being renewed by the Holy Spirit to become like the image of God, gaining again what Adam lost for himself and his offspring.

Renewal happens according to the truth of the Bible. As you come to a deep, personal knowledge of and fellowship with Christ through your study of His Word, you are renewed and refreshed. Over time, you become more and more like you were created to be.

Do not be fooled by the temptation of short cuts. There are no short cuts. God uses His Word in your life over the course of years to remake you. Remember, you have spent years being influenced and trained by a world that has rejected God. Every day you see more images and messages pushing you away from the Truth. The process of renewal takes time and God is constantly at work in your life. Trust Him. Persevere.

Verse 11 reminds you of the common heritage you have. You were lost, without hope, and in desperate need of Christ. You are much better off when you realize your shared humanity and the preeminence of Christ. As you understand your position without Christ and your identity with Christ you should be humbled. Without the work of Christ you are nothing and it is only through Him that you are who you are today. His work of renewal changes

Stephen Brazzel

your relationships, alters your prejudices, and challenges your presuppositions.

Prayer and Notes

_____

_____

_____

_____

_____

DAY 21

5/22/2024

You Are Chosen by God

Therefore, God's chosen ones, holy and loved,
put on heartfelt compassion, kindness, humility,
gentleness, and patience, (Colossians 3:12)

Because of the renewal that is taking place in your life you can live a different life, unbound from the restraints of sinfulness. Paul describes a life filled with compassion and kindness, marked by humility, gentleness, and patience. He advocates forgiveness and acceptance of others as you live in community with others who have faults also. Before we talk about this type of life and how it becomes a reality for you, we will address the quick designation Paul gives to believers.

Almost parenthetically Paul calls those who have received God's grace through faith "God's chosen ones, holy and loved." The idea of God choosing goes all the way back to at least Abraham, Isaac, and Jacob (Genesis 18:18-19; Nehemiah 9:7; Psalm 105:6; 135:4; Isaiah 41:8 and more). God chose Moses (Psalm 105:26), David (Psalm 78:70), the tribe of Judah (Psalm 78:68; 1 Chronicles 28:4), Jerusalem (1 Kings 11:36; 2 Chronicles 6:6), Solomon (1 Chronicles 28:5-7), Jeremiah (Jeremiah 1:5), Paul (Acts 9:15), and He has chosen His followers (Deuteronomy 7:6-7; John 15:16, 19; 1 Peter

67

2:9-10). This doesn't mean that you have no choice in the matter because there are plenty of passages that indicate the choice of the individual (Joshua 24:22; Judges 10:14; Psalm 119:30; John 3:18; 6:47; Ephesians 1:3 and more).

God chose first, then He was gracious to give you the opportunity to choose Him. I believe scripture teaches that God has chosen the world because of His great love (John 3:16; 2 Timothy 2:3-4; 2 Peter 3:9) but not everyone in the world will choose God. Be assured of this truth: God chose you! He wanted you! He sacrificed His own Son for you! He designed the gospel for you! You are one of His chosen ones.

You are holy and loved. When Moses was speaking to the Israelites about how God had chosen them (Deuteronomy 7:6-8) he was careful to remind them that they were not chosen for their great qualities. It wasn't because they were more numerous or better than the other nations, it was solely because He loved them. Because of His love for them, they were set apart (holy) for the purpose of God. His purpose through Israel was to use them to bring the Messiah (Jesus Christ) to the earth to pay the penalty for the entire world population. In the same way, you are loved by God and so He has made you holy through the death of His Son to bring the good news of Jesus to the world.

You weren't chosen because God was so impressed with your spiritual resume or with your outstanding talents. Remember, you were God's enemy and were spiritually dead. He chose you because He loves you. Now you are declared holy through that love. You are His chosen one.

Prayer and Notes

6|3|2021

DAY 22

You Live in God's Love

Therefore, God's chosen ones, holy and loved,
put on heartfelt compassion, kindness, humility,
gentleness, and patience, accepting one another and
forgiving one another if anyone has a complaint
against another. Just as the Lord has forgiven you,
so you must also forgive. (Colossians 3:12-13)

What does the life of a chosen, holy, loved, raised, filled, anointed, forgiven, redeemed, born again saint look like? Paul creates a list of characteristics and actions that depict a selfless life, a generous spirit, and a gracious attitude.

He begins with one of the great words in the New Testament: Compassion. The original Greek word is "splagnidzomai" which comes from the idea of the turning over of the bowels or the stomach. You might think of it as the dreadful feeling that a parent gets when they are unable to help their own child. The stomach turning over in pain as you see one you love in distress and there is nothing you can do about it. Compassion is the glory of Christianity. The world is merciless, the follower of Christ is compassionate. William Barclay wrote: It is not too much to say that everything that has been done for the aged, the sick, the weak in body and in mind, the animal, the child, the woman has been done under the inspiration of Christianity."

Kindness is shown by generous actions toward another person. These actions are intrinsically good and upright. There is no sordid motivation, only the desire to see another person supported, encouraged, and uplifted. Compassion should move you to do kind things for others.

A humble person is modest and does not try to draw attention to himself. Humility is sorely lacking in a world dominated by social media where every mild accomplishment, like ordering a milkshake, must be broadcast to the world as if a plague has just been avoided. You should examine your social media posts. Do they show humility?

Gentleness is the outpouring of a life that is meek and seeks to be considerate of others. Gentleness isn't weakness but controlling your power. Use a kind word to turn away an angry person instead of retaliating at the same volume. (Proverbs 15:1).

A patient person is only known by their patience. You cannot merely claim to be patient. You must actually be patient. Be steadfast, endure hardship, wait for God to act. Give Him time to accomplish His work in your own life as well as someone else's. Know that when you ask for patience, God will give you opportunities to be patient. These are opportunities to trust Him, to wait on Him (Psalm 27:14).

Accepting and forgiving others does not mean that you don't hold to Biblical standards. Forgiveness by definition means that a wrong has been committed. If a person has not committed a wrong against you there is no reason for forgiveness. The recognition of your own personal sin and your own personal need for forgiveness should inspire you to be gracious toward others.

Humility should make you willing to accept others with their faults. After all, you expect everyone else to accept you with your faults. Be gentle with one another, acknowledge that everyone has points of growth. Be patient with one another, God will work on you at different points and at a different rate than He will work on them. All of these work together through your life to show compassion.

Will you be compassionate? Are you so self-deluded that you think you have it all together and everyone else should bow to your superiority? Or would you like them to be compassionate towards you also? You will see someone today who needs your compassion. What will you do?

Prayer and Notes

_____

_____

_____

_____

_____

6/4/2021

DAY 23

You Are His Child

Look at how great a love the Father has given us that we should be called God's children. And we are! The reason the world does not know us is that it didn't know Him. (1 John 3:1)

Everyone who believes that Jesus is the Messiah has been born of God, and everyone who loves the Father also loves the one born of Him. This is how we know that we love God's children when we love God and obey His commands. (1 John 5:1-2)

for you are all sons of God through faith in Christ Jesus. (Galatians 3:26)

Look at how great God's love is for you. When you surrender your will to Him, He gives you the greatest gift. He adopts you as his child. Some may consider your surrender to be to a gracious but demanding dictator, but you know you are entering into a relationship with a generous and benevolent Father to whom you may cry out as his child.

Consider this description of your relationship with God today. What does it mean to be a child of God? How does a Father respond to a child? What does a child gain from a Father? If the Father knows everything, what does this mean for the child? If the Father is perfectly good and loving, what does this mean for the child? What does a good, loving Father do with a rebellious child? What does a good, loving Father desire for a child? What if the Father is also all-powerful? How does this Father expect his children to treat one another?

Each person goes through life with an individual view of fatherhood. This view is shaped in large part by your relationship with your own earthly father. What kind of man was he? Was he present? Was he involved? Was he indulgent or abusive? Was he forgiving or embittered? Was he a model to be followed or to be avoided? If your father was a good example or a bad example, your understanding of God as your Father must come from Scripture.

Whatever the relationship you had with your father, know that your heavenly Father is perfect. He is abounding in love. He is strong and tender. He is righteous and gracious. He knows what is best for you. He wants what is best for you. He is able to accomplish what is best for you. He is willing to make all things work for what is best. Even when your world may seem out of control, He is in control. He is sovereign over the entire universe.

His sovereignty does not mean that He will exempt you from hardship or from the consequences of your actions or the actions of others. It does mean that He will walk with you THROUGH the valley of the shadow of death. He will never abandon you. He will bring you to His glory one day.

As His child, you can never lose your relationship with Him. No matter what your children do, no matter how far they fall, they are always your children. As an earthly parent knows that you cannot stop loving your kids even though you may be disappointed with them and may be in despair for them. Your Father in heaven loves you more than any earthly parent ever will love their child. He was willing to sacrifice His one and only Son to bring you into His forever family. He loves you. He will never stop loving you. He will never abandon you. You are His child.

Prayer and Notes

_____

_____

_____

_____

_____

6/5/2021

DAY 24

You Have a Great Inheritance

All those led by God's Spirit are God's sons. For you did not receive a spirit of slavery to fall back into fear, but you received the Spirit of adoption, by whom we cry out, "Abba, Father!" The Spirit Himself testifies together with our spirit that we are God's children, and if children, also heirs—heirs of God and coheirs with Christ—seeing that we suffer with Him so that we may also be glorified with Him. (Romans 8:14-17)

And because you are sons, God has sent the Spirit of His Son into our hearts, crying, "Abba, Father!" So you are no longer a slave but a son, and if a son, then an heir through God. (Galatians 4:6-7)

While everyone in the world is a creation by God, not everyone is a child of God. You are a child of God by the Spirit who inhabits your life.

Paul is clear to say you are adopted into the family not purchased as a slave. The slave is afraid to do something that might make the master angry. The slave has no assurance of place, no certainty of a future. The slave lives with fear and ambiguity. The end of each day is unpredictable.

The family member has certainty. The family knows they are family no matter what may happen in the future. The relationship is sure and reliable. You are part of the family of God and can rely on that relationship to never change. You should have no fear of losing your place with the Lord.

This certainty is emphasized by the use of the phrase "coheirs with Christ." The term coheir or "joint heir" is a legal term that indicates the relationship between heirs. Coheirs are guaranteed to receive all of their inheritance individually. If any one of the coheirs does not receive the designated inheritance, then none of the coheirs is eligible to receive their inheritance. If you are a coheir with Christ then you must receive your inheritance from God or Christ will not receive His. You know that Christ will receive His, therefore you can be sure that you will receive yours.

Notice in verse 17 the inheritance includes not only glory but also suffering. Your inheritance is like that of Christ, you will be with Him in glory, but you are also assured of suffering with Him as well. Those preachers and teachers who try to sell faithfulness as the way out of suffering and into prosperity miss the truth of the gospel. Suffering doesn't mean you are out of fellowship with God, it may actually be an indication of walking in the steps of Jesus. You suffer as He did. The New Testament is pretty clear that the followers of Christ will not escape suffering (Matthew 5:10-12; 24:9; Mark 13:9; John 15:18; 1 Thessalonians 3:2-4).

Be encouraged in suffering for Christ's sake. This is a mark of your inheritance. God blesses you in the midst of the suffering. He pours out His Spirit to walk with you as you suffer. He uses the suffering to strengthen your faith and to bear witness to His grace.

When you suffer for His sake you join the legions who have gone before you in martyrdom. Suffering for Christ isn't to be sought but neither should you be reluctant to take a stand for your Father and His Son.

You are part of His family and that cannot be taken from you. You are His child and will not be abandoned. Stand firm.

Prayer and Notes

_____

_____

_____

_____

_____

6|8|2021

DAY 25

You Are Rescued

He has rescued us from the domain of darkness
and transferred us into the kingdom of the Son He
loves. We have redemption, the forgiveness of sins,
in Him. (Colossians 1:13-14)

Redemption is one of the great words of the Bible. In common usage, it often loses significance because of the context in which it is used. Ball players redeem themselves when they make a good play after having made a bone headed play. Politicians try to redeem themselves after having made a poor decision or a personally detrimental statement. Most of the time the word redemption is used reflexively, "we need to redeem ourselves."

In scripture, redemption is not used reflexively but passively. Instead of you redeeming yourself, you are redeemed by God. The matter requiring redemption is no mere poor decision or bad play, but your own actions of rebellion and trespass. The work of redemption is not merely God making a better play or doing something to make you look better, it is Him giving His Son who poured out His blood for your redemption.

Redemption is a big deal. And the scripture says that you are redeemed! This is monumental.

In order for someone to be redeemed out of slavery, a price must be paid. There were 60 million slaves in the Roman Empire, and often they were bought and sold like pieces of furniture. A slave could be redeemed if someone were willing to pay the purchase price and then set the slave free. This is what Jesus did for you. He paid the price of your slavery by going to the cross and dying in your place. Having done so, He then set you free by forgiving your sin.

Rescue, transfer, and forgiveness are the immediate results of your redemption.

Paul says you are rescued from the domain of darkness. This is the domain where you lived as a slave to sin. You had no option to please God because you were spiritually dead. When you accepted the work of God through Christ you were rescued from this domain. You no longer live in darkness, you are in the light.

Brought out of the darkness, you were transferred into His kingdom. You are now in the kingdom of God. You don't have to wait to go to heaven to experience the kingdom, you live in the kingdom today. You are a child of the king. You experience the freedom of the kingdom. You were deported from the domain of darkness into the kingdom of light. What an amazing thing to go from a place of bondage, darkness, and hopelessness into a place of light, joy, and freedom.

You should note also the verbs here are past tense verbs. They denote a completed action on your behalf. This is a permanent move. You cannot go back. This is completed action. This is redemption.

God has taken you out of a terrible place and has brought you into a wonderful place. Imagine the joy the Israelites had as they were rescued from Egypt and transferred into the freedom of the Promised Land. Unfortunately as you read the accounts in Exodus, Numbers, and Deuteronomy it becomes clear that at times they wanted to go back to the safety of their slavery in Egypt. Resist the temptation to desire the slavery of sin. Enjoy where God has placed you today. It is a good thing to be free, to be redeemed.

Prayer and Notes

_____

_____

_____

_____

_____

DAY 26

6/9/2021

You Are Redeemed

> We have redemption in Him through His blood,
> the forgiveness of our trespasses, according to the
> riches of His grace that He lavished on us with
> all wisdom and understanding. (Ephesians 1:7-8)

Redemption is entirely the result of the boundless love of God toward you. You are redeemed "according to the riches of His grace." There are no bounds to this grace. There is no sin He will not forgive. There is no trespass for which His blood will not atone. There is no act of rebellion too great for His love to wash you clean.

Even as you have gone through these days of devotion, you may still have thoughts of something in your past. You may still think your past is too dark even for God to forgive. You may still remind yourself of the depth of your rebellion and you may still consider yourself too unworthy for God's grace.

Let's talk about your sin for a moment. You need to agree on a couple of things. First you must agree that your emotion cannot overrule your mind. If you are going to be ruled by your emotions then it will be very difficult for you to accept the truth of the gospel message. Second, you must agree that God's word will be the final and ultimate truth for you. If you will not accept His word as the ultimate truth then you have placed your own thoughts above the Bible and there is no way for you to move past whatever you think about yourself.

Remembering your sin does not mean that your sin has not been forgiven. Just because you remember your own sin doesn't mean that it was not redeemed through His blood. Sometimes God allows you to remember your sin and the pain of it to keep you from going back to it. However, you should not allow your remembrance of it become your truth. The scripture says that you have been forgiven according to the riches of His grace that are lavished on you. He has forgiven it all. He has done so knowing exactly what your sin is. He has done so knowing exactly how depraved you were. He is not without wisdom or understanding. Yet He has chosen to forgive your sin. You need to let it go.

At the root of the word forgive is the idea of letting go. God removes your sin from your life and He lets it go. He takes it upon Himself and then lets it go. You should too. Satan loves for you to consistently remember your past so that he can use it to keep you from moving forward. God is not reminding you of your past. God is calling you to follow Him as He goes forward. Over time, your sin will have less hold of your memory as you consistently let it go and stand in God's redemption and forgiveness.

Redemption also means that God is able to take your mistakes and your sin, your past and your darkness, and use it to His glory. This is the ultimate work of redemption when that which was your shame becomes God's glory. Some of the most beautiful examples of God's redemption come from those whose lives were deeply wrecked by addictions. God often uses those lives to bring a message of hope to others who feel trapped by their own cycle of sin. God will redeem your past by allowing you to draw from it in ministry to others.

When you remember that it is God alone who put you in this good place, who redeemed your life from the pit, you can become a powerful witness to others who are looking for a way out. God's great love for you should open your eyes to His love for others who are walking a similar path. He can use your story of redemption to give someone else hope.

Prayer and Notes

_____

_____

_____

_____

_____

6/13/2021

DAY 27

You Are Anointed by the Holy Spirit

> But you have an anointing from the Holy One, and
> all of you have knowledge, I have not written to
> you because you don't know the truth, but because
> you do know it, and because no lie comes from the
> truth. (1 John 2:21-21)

> When you heard the message of truth, the gospel
> of your salvation, and when you believed in Him,
> you were also sealed with the promised Holy
> Spirit. He is the down payment of our inheritance,
> for the redemption of the possession, to the praise
> of His glory. (Ephesians 1:13-14)

> Now it is God who strengthens us, with you, in
> Christ and has anointed us. He has also sealed us
> and given us the Spirit as a down payment in our
> hearts. (2 Corinthians 1:21-22)

John the disciple writes this letter to those who are believers
and who are going through various challenges to their faith. He
wants them to be sure of their salvation and to know what that
salvation means. There were some wannabe theologians bringing

false teachings into the church and causing some to doubt the simple gospel message. John warns the believers of false teachers and even "antichrists." These antichrists are simply those who are teaching "against Christ." How would they know? How can they discern the truth?

The simple promise of the gospel is that all those who are believers in Christ have "an anointing from the Holy One." This anointing is the presence of the Holy Spirit. This is the Holy Spirit of God promised by Jesus, the Spirit of Truth (John 14:16-17, 26; 16:13). As a believer, the Holy Spirit is in you from the moment of faith. He seals you for eternity. He is the deposit made by God to give evidence of your redemption. He is the same Spirit who anointed Jesus Himself (Acts 10:38).

You do not become a god when you are saved, but you receive the presence of God into your life. The Holy Spirit bears witness to your inner spirit that you are saved and He leads you into all knowledge. You don't automatically become a Ph.D. in theology, but you now have within you the light of truth who will lead you into all truth as you study God's Word and strive to honor Him with your life.

You can discern the truth from the lies because you have the Spirit of Truth in your life. You can understand the scripture because you have the Spirit of the writer of scripture in your life. You still need to study, ponder, work, and meditate to learn. God chooses to cause you to dig for the truth, but you now have a witness within to guide you into the truth.

This same Spirit is also called the Comforter in John 14. It is the Spirit of God who embodies the presence of God in your life and from whom you receive the "peace of God, which surpasses every thought" (Philippians 4:7). It is the Spirit who comforts as you "walk through the valley of the shadow of death" (Psalm 23:4). It is the Spirit who makes you strong when pressured, wise when perplexed, bold when persecuted, and helps you survive when struck down (2 Corinthians 4:8-9).

This Spirit is in you, anoints you for the work of God by the power of God. This same Spirit was in Abraham, Moses, David, Isaiah, Jeremiah, Ezekiel, Samuel, Elisha, and Jesus. And He is in you.

Prayer and Notes

_____

_____

_____

_____

_____

DAY 28

6/15/2021

You Are a New Creation

> Therefore if anyone is in Christ, there is a new creation; old things have passed away, and look, new things have come. (2 Corinthians 5:17)

Christians are not reformed, rehabilitated, or reeducated—they are recreated. When you were converted by God, you didn't merely turn over a new leaf or get a fresh start, you began a brand new life. The old was gone, the new came in like a storm. The old selfish, sinful, darkness filled life ended. Old ways of thinking, doing, and talking were abolished. A new life began. One commentator puts it this way: "If anyone is in Christ (boom!) new creation."

To be "in Christ" means to be united to Christ by faith. One of Paul's favorite phrases, "in Christ" describes more than a location, it is a relationship that overwhelms all other prior relationships. Jesus describes it in John 15 as being the branch in a vine. United to the vine, the branch derives all its nourishment from the vine. The branch is supported by the vine. The branch is sustained by the vine. The branch has no identity apart from the vine.

Those who are in Christ, who are united to Christ, are now new creations. The old has gone and the new has come. This means that you undergo a complete change in worldview, feelings, emotions, values, goals, and morals. You are not the same person; you are new.

The gospel is powerful. The gospel completely changes you. When God looks at your life He doesn't look at a better version of who you were, He sees a brand new person. He sees you as He created you to be. He sees you as He designed you to be.

To take this new person and go back to living as if you were the same old person is foolishness. That is not who you are anymore. Your life is different now because of all that God has done and because of His presence in your life as the Holy Spirit. Don't fall back into old habits. Don't allow old ways to pollute your new life. Don't spend a moment longing for the old days when you were walking in darkness.

Set your heart on things above. Strive for those higher, nobler things that you are now capable of doing. Fill your soul with the joy of forgiveness and obedience. Live as a freedom lover who knows the God of the universe. Be gracious to others. Extend mercy to those in need of mercy. Love God with abandon. Rest in His abounding love for you. This is your life now. You are a brand new creation, just like He meant for you to be.

Prayer and Notes

_____

_____

_____

_____

6/16/2024

DAY 29

You are His People

> But you are a chosen race, a royal priesthood,
> a holy nation, a people for His possession,
> so that you may proclaim the praises
> of the One who called you out of darkness
> into His marvelous light.
> Once you were not a people,
> but now you are God's people;
> you had not received mercy,
> but now you have received mercy. (1 Peter 2:9-10)

Your existence with God is more than just as an individual. In 1 Peter, the apostle describes the church and those in the church as "living stones" (v. 5) and then as a "chosen race, a royal priesthood, a holy nation, a people for His possession." Together with other believers you have an identity. You are with other believers in the universal Church and also in a local embodiment of the local church. Those who claim the universal Church and reject the local church are misreading the New Testament and rejecting the plan of God for the world. You should never entertain the idea that you can be absolved from membership and activity in a local church.

He has chosen you (read this as a plural you, "Y'all" for those in Texas). Because of His love, He chose you together to fulfill His plan. Once used for the people of Israel, now this designation is for Jews and Gentiles alike under the banner of Jesus Christ.

You all are a royal priesthood and a holy priesthood (v. 5). He isn't just speaking to a special class of believers who should take the spiritual leadership of a church, but of all believers. You are a priest before God. The role of a priest can be described by two roles: Represent God before the people and represent the people before God. As a member of the royal priesthood, you are called to let people know about God and to speak to them about the desires and plans God has for them. You are also responsible for going to God on behalf of the people in prayer. Beseech God on their behalf. Call out to Him for those who don't yet know Him.

You are together a holy nation. As the people of God on earth, you are part of the kingdom of God and so represent the plan of God for eternity. As citizens of heaven, you should be united and present through that unity a vision of the grace and mercy of God. This doesn't mean that all Christians should be members of one church or that there is no place for denominations within the nation of Christianity or that all believers should form their own political party. It means as a unified body under the banner of Christ you must be gracious to one another, accepting one another as Christ accepted you (Romans 15:7). Don't get so carried away with the faults of others that you begin to think you have no faults. Be gracious.

You are a people for His possession. The old King James Version translated this phrase "a peculiar people." The church is certainly made up of peculiar people. It is clearer to say that you are His possession. The demarcation of ownership is important. You belong to Him. You are not your own. You are His. His special possession. Before you were not a people, but now you belong to Him.

This is who you are. This is who you are together. You are living stones that God is building into a spiritual house to offer your lives as sacrifices to Him. You can only fulfill God's plan for the world when you live together in community, part of a local church, accepting one another, and encouraging one another. It is among that group of called out ones where you learn to extend grace and accept grace.

Prayer and Notes

_____

_____

_____

_____

_____

6|17|202~

DAY 30

This is What You Call Yourself

Here is a summary of passages related to identity. This isn't an exhaustive list, but one that you can use to remind yourself of the things God has done for you and declared about you. His truth about you needs to overwhelm you. Every day you will receive messages that counter this truth. Immerse yourself in His truth and allow it to become your truth about yourself. It can be helpful to read this list every day or every week for a while to let it sink in to your heart.

John 1:12	I am a child of God (Romans 8:16; 1 John 3:1)
John 15:1, 5	I am a part of the true vine, a branch of His life
John 15:15	I am Christ's friend
John 15:16	I am chosen and appointed by Christ to bear His fruit
Romans 3:24	I have been justified and redeemed
Romans 5:1	I have been justified and am at peace with God
Romans 6:1-6	I died with Christ and died to the power of sin's rule in my life
Romans 6:7	I have been freed from sin's power over me
Romans 8:1	I am free from condemnation
Romans 8:14-15	I am a child of God (Galatians 3:26)

93

Romans 8:17	I am an heir of God and coheir with Christ
Romans 11:16	I am holy
Romans 15:7	I am accepted by Christ
1 Corinthians 1:2	I have been sanctified
1 Corinthians 2:12	I have received the Spirit of God into my life
1 Corinthians 3:16; 6:19	I am a temple of God; His Spirit dwells in me
1 Corinthians 6:19-20	I have been bought with a price. I belong to God.
1 Corinthians 12:27	I am a member of Christ's body
2 Corinthians 1:21	I have been anointed by God
2 Corinthians 5:17	I am a new creation
2 Corinthians 5:21	I am the righteousness of God in Christ
Galatians 2:20	I have been crucified with Christ and now Christ lives in me
Galatians 3:26, 28	I am a child of God and one in Christ
Galatians 4:6-7	I am a child of God and a coheir with Christ
Ephesians 1:1	I am a saint
Ephesians 1:3	I am blessed with every spiritual blessing
Ephesians 1:4	I was chosen in Christ before the foundation of the world to be holy and without blame before Him
Ephesians 1:5	I have been adopted as God's child
Ephesians 1:7-8	I have been redeemed and forgiven
Ephesians 2:5	I have been made alive with Christ
Ephesians 2:6	I have been raised up and seated with Christ
Ephesians 2:10	I am God's workmanship
Ephesians 2:19	I am a fellow citizen with the saints and a member of God's household
Ephesians 3:6	I am a coheir with Christ
Ephesians 4:24	I am righteous and holy
Philippians 3:20	I am a citizen of heaven
Colossians 1:13	I have been delivered from the domain of darkness and transferred to the kingdom of Christ
Colossians 1:14	I have been redeemed and forgiven

Colossians 2:7	I have been firmly rooted in Christ
Colossians 2:10	I have been made complete in Christ
Colossians 2:12-13	I have been buried, raised and made alive with Christ and totally forgiven
Colossians 3:1	I have been raised with Christ
Colossians 3:3	I have been hidden with Christ
Colossians 3:4	Christ is now my life
Colossians 3:12	I am chosen of God, holy and dearly loved
1 Thessalonians 5:5	I am a child of light and not of darkness
2 Timothy 1:7	I have been given a spirit of power, love and discipline
2 Timothy 1:9	I have been saved and called
Hebrews 4:16	I may come boldly before the throne of Christ
1 Peter 2:5	I am a living stone being built into a spiritual house
1 Peter 2:9-10	I am part of a chosen race, a royal priesthood, a holy nation, a people of God's own possession
1 John 3:1	I am a child of God, dearly loved
1 John 4:15	God is in me and I am in God

Made in the USA
Coppell, TX
24 September 2020